WORK YOUR WORDS

Finding Your Pathway To Personal Success

Andrew E. Guy

Copyright © 2014 by Andrew E. Guy

First editions: published and printed
in 2014 under the following ISBNs

Published January 2014
ISBN 978-0-7414-7162-8 (SC)
ISBN 978-0-7414-7163-5 (HC)
ISBN 978-0-7414-7164-2 (eBook)

New Edition: Reprinted
Published January 2015

GLADSHARE MEDIA PUBLISHING

ISBN 978-1-987890-01-3 (SC)
ISBN 978-1-987890-02-0 (eBook)

Printed in the United States of America

GLADSHARE
MEDIA
PUBLISHING

INFO@GLADSHAREMEDIA.COM
WWW.GLADSHAREMEDIA.COM
WWW.GLADSHAREPUBLISHING.COM

CONTENTS

DEDICATION

To my two "Dudes", Therand and Alin, for without you guys, the true meaning of living would have surpassed me. You are off to an early start on your pathways to success. I am so proud of you!

To all my students and the faculty members in the DCPS community, may you find real success beyond words in everything you do.

To everyone who's ever had a dream, and wondered if it was possible. I am here to tell you yes, all things are possible!

Finally, to my loyal audience at www.Andrewguyspeaks.com, success is possible...

ENDORSEMENTS

According to Webster's dictionary success is "the progressive realization of a worthwhile goal or dream." In this book Andrew has done a fantastic job working with the reader to help them understand that success is a "journey not a destination." Anyone can achieve it but you must be able to understand the progress and work for it. It is an easy motivational read that makes you want to take action.

Dave Oakes, Speaker, Trainer
owner-Dave Oakes Seminars

"The power of words cannot be understated, written or not. Andrew shows us the path should we choose it, at a time when self-doubt prevents us from working our words and achieving what at times seems impossible."

Tasneem Hashmi, MSc
Assistant Center Manager
FlightSafety International

"This book is a must read to remind each of us to continue to "Watch our Mouths!" In a child's world, we are "Dream Makers, Dream Breakers or Dream Crushers". Determine today, to *"Watch what we say"* and encourage a child to "Make his Dream" become *TRUTH*."

Mrs. V. Forshee
Former Assistant Principal
Northwestern and Ribault Middle Schools
Duval County Public Schools, Jacksonville, Florida

"Growing up in a strong Christian family I always thought life would be good and fair if I did the right things. At almost 60, I have learned that I cannot control people, but only my response to how people manage their situations. Personal reaction can either be a stumbling block, or a testimony to my faith. It takes a true heart of God to consistently respond in a Godly way. Andrew has a true heart for God."

Gary S Glover
Medevac Pilot
CW5 US Army (Ret).

ACKNOWLEDGMENTS

This project would never have been possible without the encouragement and support of many people I've been blessed with along the pathway to discovering my gifts.

To my wonderful wife, Theresa, for all your hard work and patience over the years. Thank you for entertaining my "B.I.G." thoughts as I dreamed out loud. You sacrifice so much, including your beauty sleep as I stay up all night typing with the lights on. Thank you Sweetie.

To my loving mother, Una Guy, who simply said "HEAVEN, YES and HELL, NO! And who, through her faith in God found her pathway to success as she overcame hard times and persevered for the love of her children. Had it not been for you, life itself would not have been possible. To my dad, Doran Guy for being a vessel of support over the years.

To my "B.I.G." brother Courtney, owner of (*CG Catering Service)* and the greatest chef on this side of heaven. Thank you for always being a manly example and the inspiration that kept me believing during the tough times. And to my God-sent father, Mr. Rupert Blackwood, who took the function of fatherhood to another level. As you reflect on these words, I pray this book will be a blessing to your eyes, heart and mind for the many sacrifices you made for me.

To Deanne "Mama Dee" and Mitch Goldman, thank you for welcoming me into your family. Your unconditional love and support inspires me deeply.

To Mr. Gary S. Glover, thank you for your invaluable support over the years to my family and me. Among other things, you became my mentor and truly exemplified how to "Work Your Words".

To Grandmaster Cocker and Master James C. Lamoureux of *Yesha* Tae Kwondo Ministries, for allowing me to develop my skills in martial arts and pour into the lives of the students.

To all those who have advised, encouraged and tolerated me in any way, thank you.

To the creator of all things, the God of my salvation of whose banner over me is love. You are the ultimate example of success and the pathway through which every process of living becomes meaningful.

INTRODUCTION

Words create everything visible and invisible—"Let there be..." and there it was... the universe!

Words are powerful so be mindful of what you say. Words are a result of everything our senses reveal to us. Like an atom, words are the raw material and building blocks of everything, "matter." They are the thread of yesterday, the fabric of today and the clothing of our tomorrow—the *future* that awaits us at the end of our thinking. Your words begin with thoughts but end with work.

This book is designed to encourage and motivate you to dream, think, become inspired, and then work the words you speak to create the world want. As you read this book I hope you will discover and be convinced that you can have what you say, do what you think, follow your dreams and live what you desire. You don't need a PhD to change your life, just desire. So be encouraged. Scientists say that humans use less than ten percent of their brains, but it has been my dream to write a book that will stimulate the world to attempt to use the other ninety percent within your lifetime. Take the limits off your limitations and create a greater world, starting with yourself then your home, community, society and country.

Always remember, success has a pathway that leads to a destiny that awaits you. But to reach your destiny you must be willing to change, adapt and work to make your words a reality. This book is filled with stories, examples, tips and powerful quotes to help you along your path to personal success. Therefore, I encourage you to use this book as a resource for each transition along the way.

In a world where change is a discomfort and the processes of adjusting to unforeseen events are seldom understood, change is our most constant reminder that the process of living is one of determination, triumph, and new beginnings. Change is the answer to a stagnated nation, where failures become "lessons-learned" and growth enables us to expand our thinking to reach past our emotions and beyond our wildest imaginations.

Growth is a necessary component that makes living worth the gift of life. The lack thereof, makes you a prime candidate for permanent extinction. However, to grow you must learn; and to learn is to discover pathways to your success. The choice is yours, so make it a growth one.

We are products of success, and we must function as such. Furthermore, there can be no success outside the will of the creator of all things, God. Therefore, the success of a product is only possible when it functions according to the specifications of its maker. You are successfully created to be a success. While success can be enjoyed as a group, real success is first personal before it becomes public. As a result, personal success is important to your ongoing motivation and desire to live. But before any success can become personal or public, it requires working your words. Simple talk will not do what dedicated work, time and perseverance will accomplish—the impossible! So read on...then get out there and WORK YOUR WORDS!

CHAPTER ONE

W.O.R.K. THE REAL YOU: The personality of success

*"Success compels us to dream BIG—BIG enough
that the life of the dreamer will change
significantly should the dream
ever become a reality."*
~Andrew E. Guy

NOTES

> *"The heights by great men reached and kept were not attained by sudden flight, but they, while their companions slept, were toiling upward in the night."*
> **~Longfellow, Henry Wadsworth**

Despite what you've been told, it is not some event that happens in the distant future; success is work, it's you, and it is here now. Are there things you've always wanted to do, places you wish you could go? You have everything inside of you to make it happen. Success is an internal operation that has a built-in mechanism that craves the application of new knowledge after it has been discovered. It is not a onetime event that happens in your life; real success is a ***"Total-Freedom-Mindset"*** that empowers you to make every moment of living count and to effectively accomplish any task you set out to do daily. Success is not idle talk; it requires action. In fact, simple talk gets you nowhere, fast. Hence, the title of this book: Work Your Words. One hundred percent of success starts and ends with ***W.O.R.K,*** and the good news is that it is available to anyone who is willing and prepared to pursue it.

There's a freedom of living that awaits you, it's called success.

When I speak of WORK I am talking about a mindset that has:

W - Willingness with empowerment to go the extra mile to do the things others fail to do; to welcome strangers into your heart, and to perpetually work on making yourself the greatest you that this world has ever seen.

O - Obligation to the trailblazers who came ahead of you and left invaluable principles for you to follow. It takes a special person to discover the freedom that comes with true success. Beyond personality, success requires you to have a high aptitude of passion for application of your giftedness and compassion for the advancement of people, not just you.

R - Reliability to be consistent with a strong hope that you will never quit, even when quitting gives up on you.

K - Knowledge that is renewable and ever expanding your mind to develop yourself to a higher level of personal growth.

> *"When work, commitment, and pleasure all become one and you reach that deep well where passion lives, nothing is impossible."*
> *~Author unknown*

Aside from work, you must know that everything in life has with it a personality that defines, separates, classifies and identifies some visual aspects of characteristics that sets it apart from other such things. I call this *"The Power Of Differentiation."* In the same manner, people might differ in their thinking but we all want the same thing, the pursuit of happiness and the power to transform our lives for the better. Success is no different; it requires work, it is specific; it is tangible and therefore, requires you to think differently to achieve it.

As the extension of an individual, success is the packaged ingredient that makes you unique and extremely unforgettable. You are too unique to be overlooked, and far too amazing to be forgotten. You are an original and there is no carbon copy of you out there.

Moreover, like a fingerprint, there is only one assigned to each person. Because of this, you have a success personality that is unlike any other. Therefore, no one can do what you do, like you do, when you do what you do, one hundred percent, wholeheartedly. I call this an "orig-o-pen-dinal" (an original who is open to the gift of life and process of living).

THE ROLE OF CONFIDENCE

One of the traits of success is sheer confidence. Not cocky or self-indulging mannerisms, but the type of confidence that permeates the very fibers of ones being and one that is so contagious that everyone who comes in contact with you is positively impacted and affected forever. To put this into a clearer perspective, if you are not transforming lives you are not living, you are simply existing and taking up needful space.

Confidence therefore, is not what others think of you. It is how you see yourself in this world, and above all, the things you say to yourself on a daily basis. Are you an over-comer? Then, say it! Are you gifted in something (even if you have not discovered it yet) then say, I am a gift waiting to be discovered and the world will see me in a different way today!

Are you healthy, strong, and empowered to use your today (the now) to redesign the molecules of negativism into a more positive, productive tomorrow (the then)? Then, say it for screaming-out-load! I can and I will, even if it takes me a lifetime to do what I must do and do it like an **"orig-o-pen-dinal,"** like no one else can do, when I do what I do, one hundred percent, wholeheartedly! Say it loud! Say it proud! Then after you've said it, take action and work your words like nobody's business and make it happen. And keep it moving forward...

Living is about forward thinking, and true success is motivated and fueled by this kind of thought process. In the same light, confidence will be the momentum that pushes you into your greatness. Again, do not abandon your confidence; in fact, work on improving it daily. Why? Because confidence allows you to attain what you are created to do thereby enabling you to positively impact lives.

FAITH THAT WORKS

Yes, I said FAITH. And no, it has nothing to do with religion. Actually, faith is a pathway of living that makes life possible. W.O.R.K. THE REAL YOU!

You must believe to achieve. I don't care how you fix it, twist it, bend it, fold it or measure it; you must believe! Nothing great just happens by luck or by chance. Hence, the myth of the "Big Bang Theory" still remains a mystery today.

Faith is at the helm of every achievement visible and invisible, while believing is the action whereby all realities are manifested.

Everyone who has ever accomplished anything in living is, and will always be a dreamer who believed and took the necessary actions to make it a reality. You may look at reality as the awareness that all things are possible. When you believe this, you become unstoppable because you will begin to put actions to your words. Don't just talk and gibber-jabber, work your words.

DREAMS AND REALITY

If you are alive you are a success; however, this type of success is what I call **"Given-Success."** But the success that is significant, transcending, and life-changing is a result of you embracing all of the experiences you encounter in life. This takes work. In other words you may say, why did those things happen to me? The hurt, pains, setbacks, disappointments, and discomforts? Why me? And how can I use them to improve my life, family, community, neighborhood, and surroundings? I call this **"Earned-Success."** Failures are stepping-stones to greatness if they become lessons-learned for growth and continual self-improvement.

In the movie Ratatouille, Chef Gusto, said *"Anyone Can Cook."* The same is true to living as it applies to personal success. Anyone can be successful, but not everyone can manage success.

To be successful you must plan to embrace change, and in order for you to embrace unforeseen changes, you must have a plan for living. As you'll learn later, there's a major difference between life and living. One is a gift, and the other is a process.

While a plan is the beginning of your success, what you do is more vital to the realities of living. Therefore, action is the cornerstone to making every plan a reality.

In the end every personal success begins with reality. Any success that is not realized is only a dream that will never become a reality.

I call this a **"pipe-dream"** that will forever remain in the tunnels of your sub-conscience and never see the light of the real day. Success requires action; it must be translated into something real that transforms the lives of people. Ever heard the saying, keep it real? Well, the same goes for your personal success, MAKE IT REAL—the reality that will perpetually motivate you even in the toughest of times. When the friends are gone, the car won't start, and lights are off because you didn't pay the bill, hang in there and keep on believing.

> "No amount of reading or memorizing will make you successful in life. It is the understanding and application of wise thought which counts."
> (Bob Proctor, author of You Were Born Rich)

Success compels us to dream, but not just any dream; it must be BIG—BIG enough that the life of the dreamer will change significantly should the dream ever become a reality. There is no room for small dreams. Most people will tell you the sky is the limit, but I disagree. There is no limit to what you can think, do and accomplish before you hit the grave. You are not limited by circumstances, but how you think. You are not a failure for what you do, but how you think.

So hang your dreams past the sky. Go to space if you have to. That way if you fall, you're still in the air, way up high where the eagles of success soar effortlessly. The universe is waiting for dreams like yours; and there is still room at the top.

But imagine this also, not dreaming is like having a ton of heavy lead strapped to your ankles as you hang above a million tons of electrically charged iron grids with gigantic sharp spikes screaming "BLOODY FAILURE!" waiting for you to fall as they glitter with vicious hunger—and the closer you are to earth, the faster and harder you fall. Your success is no different. The "haters" are like the sharp iron grids waiting for you to fall, and they will come out of the "woodworks" to see it come to fruition. Never mind their temporary distractions to your lifelong success. You have to ignore them.

You don't have to be a Nike fan to understand this simple concept, **"Just Do It!"** It is far better to die trying (for this is living) than to die not trying anything at all (for this is the real tragedy). Think of it this way. If you were convinced that all dreams come true, what would you dream of? Wouldn't you dream of something so great that it would take you a lifetime to see it come to pass? "Darn-skippy" you would. I know I would, and I am doing just that. Keep reading... This is what success is all about, dreaming bigger than your brain can consume, longer than life will sustain, deeper than any ocean, and farther than any river can run.

Mind you, dreaming was not meant for the brain but for the mind because the mind is by far a lot bigger than your brain. And while the brain is only a confined lump of matter that weighs about three pounds, the mind has no boundaries, it remains weightless, unrestricted, infinitely powerful, and relentlessly flexible. The personality of success is mental and embodies everything that exist today and those to come. There's more, keep reading...

THE NEED FOR OTHERS

Every one of us is a type of vessel made to serve each other in our own unique and gifted way. This wonderful process is set into motion when you start to speak, believe, then work what you say to make the invisible your personal reality. Remember, everyone hears, but not everyone listens; therefore, your thoughts become visible by your words, and intentions are only made visible through the things you do. If you don't do something, someone else will; so you are better off doing it anyway. Here's a tip that will guide you through living, (say less, see more, hear all...just listen and you'll learn far more than you think). The strange thing is that something always happens, even if you do nothing. The brighter solution to this is that you are able to determine what happens to you.

Although you can do great things, however, a major factor in all of this is that you cannot do it alone; you will need others to help you along the way. Like the process of hand washing. Through lathering and rinsing one hand washes the other and they both become clean. Think of yourself as one of the hands holding the soap of opportunities, of which are many, and the people you meet and create lasting relationships with are the ones who help you lather up, scrub, rinse and dry.

Even though success is first personal before it becomes public, this principle remains; you need others. While things like fashion will fade away, people will always be there, providing they are the right ones. You might ask, "If people are so important in the grand scheme of success, where do I place money?" My answer to this is very simple; money should always be a servant and a subservient commodity to people. It is people that make the world go around, not money. For example, if you leave a one hundred dollar bill in the middle of Time Square, New York, all things held constant, (and there are no sticky fingers within a one million mile radius of that bill), it will remain there unused, untouched, undeveloped and without growth. Unless a human with a success mindset puts this one hundred dollar bill into productive action, nothing will happen. Bottom line, it is vital that you see people as an essential part of your pathway to personal success.

By discovering your pathway and then working your words to create what you speak, you will become the ladder that provides the steps for others to follow, discover, and be transformed forever. Therefore, it is vital that you do your part.

> *"I want to be remembered*
> *for what I've left behind."*
> ~Lennex Lewis.

FROM PERSONAL TO PUBLIC

Success is everything that is inside of you and waits for you to discover it. The personality of success is a personal freedom that is first personal then it becomes public. For most people, this is the reverse. They seek out public success before personal. This leads to self-destruction and ill-gained accomplishments, which are made on the backs of others. The problem arises when most people lose themselves in the process, having little or no self-image, unstable and without self-sustainability. They eventually become dependent on or burdensome to others.

Public success is driven by low self-esteem. So be mindful of this approach. You will be much more equipped if you first develop yourself, set your standards high, and create personal boundaries that will protect you as you navigate your pathway to personal success.

Any person who has ever achieved genuine public success, first did it personally. For this reason, you must always look inwards for your success before looking outward or anywhere else. You must then manage yourself in order to remain consistent with your priorities and set realistic goals. Unlike the many books written on the subject of time management, I am here to tell you that success has little to do with time or the management of it. However, it is the sincere control of self that regulate the processes of living and empowers people to do extraordinary things. True success is only possible because of self-management, and not time.

DEALING WITH CHANGE

Sometimes finding your path to success involves climbing your way out of a bad situation to obtain something better. Sometimes it involves working hard on a good situation to make it better. But no matter where you are on your path to success you will have to deal with change at some points in your life. By far change is quite a challenge for all of us. And no one masters change; you either become better at it or it gets the best of you. If you are not mindful, change may consume you.

Change is a critical component of living that forces us to abandon sedentary thinking for a lifestyle of movement and action. Like dreaming change is never boxed-in. It is free and flexible. It transcends cultures, time, religion, dogmas and paradigms, and it is no respecter of persons. We are all affected by change. It is a way of life and a pathway to experiencing the freedom of personal success. Change is biologically embedded in our DNA (deoxyribonucleic acids), and in our psyches.

John Kotter along with co-author Holger Rathgeber, wrote in the famous book *"Our Iceberg is Melting."* It is about the ability to recognize, adapt and respond to change. The book, written as a fable, is centered around a colony of emperor penguins who live on an iceberg in Antarctica. Their home is a huge iceberg that one of their fellow penguins believes is melting. Although some of the "sedentary-thinking" penguins grew accustomed to their ways of living and saw no need for change, some of the leaders were able to rally the colony to swift action that led to their migration to a better iceberg.

In the same light, many of us are apathetic to change. We just like things to remain the way they are, just like some of these Antarctic-dwelling penguins. The strange thing about change is that it requires our full participation for the processes of living to take their natural course. The same is also true about success; it has a personality that will not always identify with others who neglect change. According to the authors, "if you handle the process of change well, you can prosper greatly, but handle it poorly, and you put yourself and others at risk" (J. Kotter, H. Rathgeber 2005).

Another fable that epitomizes the lesson of change is *"Who Moved My Cheese"* by Dr. Spencer Johnson, M.D. In his popular book, he metaphorically uses a "Maze" as a representation of the real world. In this maze, Dr. Johnson places four characters that would live out the process of change to illustrate how people are affected by their willingness, or the lack of it, to effectively respond to change.

According to Dr. Spencer, there are seven signs of change that everyone should recognize and respond to. This very important list below includes the keys to unlocking the pathway to your personal success as it relates to change.

- *"Change Happens (They Keep Moving The Cheese);*
- *Anticipate Change (Get Ready For The Cheese To Move);*
- *Monitor Change (Smell The Cheese often So You Know When It Is Getting Old);*
- *Adapt To Change Quickly (The Quicker You Let Go Of old Cheese, The Sooner you Can Enjoy New Cheese);*
- *Change (Move With The Cheese);*
- *Enjoy Change (Savor The Adventure And Enjoy The Taste Of New Cheese);*
- *Be Ready To Change Quickly And Enjoy It Again & Again (They Keep Moving The Cheese)*

~Spencer Johnson, M.D. 1998."

POINTS TO PONDER

Success is waiting on you. Do not think it is for anyone else but you. Like a life-changing opportunity, success has a limited lifespan, and you must seize it within its lifetime. We are all capable of achieving personal success, however, it is the path taken that determines the difference between those who make it and others who do not.

Most people will argue with you until the cows come home, go to bed, and wake up again— that success is out there, somewhere, and that you have to spend your entire life chasing after it, like some runaway dish without a spoon. Hold up...Wait a minute...That's not true success. I call this an oppressive burden that speeds up your time toward the open grave. The entire process is stress-driven, oppression-centered, glory-seeking, self-indulgent, and greed-focused.

On the contrary, like your personality, you must discover your own success from within and then find the right path that will allow you to manifest the invisible (what is inside of you) into a visible reality where you live, work, and play. Where you live is the place where you are most at peace; where you work is where you serve your gift to the world, and where you play is entirely up to you, but it is a process of celebration that comes to help you cope with the nuances of living.

As you think about your life and the choices you've made, the people you've met or haven't, and the places you've gone or those you wish to one day visit, I want you to ponder what success really means to you.

I want you to imagine, what it looks, feels, and tastes like; where it is and how do you find the right pathway that gets you there.

CHAPTER TWO

ESTABLISHING YOUR BRAND

...Rediscovering the real you

*"When you don't know where you're going,
any road will get your there"
(Dr. Myles Munroe)*

NOTES

Rediscovering the real you require more than just a brief look in the mirror every now and again. In fact, it requires a willingness to question, to let go of the dark pasts and to embrace a brighter future. It calls for an indelible self-branding of your personal success, a type of success that will pave the way for the next generation to come. While easier said than done, most of us desperately hope that someone would rediscover us and show us the way. In most cases, sometimes it is necessary to seek external aid, but you'll never be externally discovered until you become internally uncovered.

Personal discovery is the total acceptance of self. There will never be an identity crisis when you truly know who you are. The downfall to lack of self-knowledge is low self-esteem, poor self-image, lack of confidence, unfilled dreams, untapped potential, and a congested graveyard fertile with dead bodies of wounded souls. Self-knowledge is paramount to personal success.

We have been so out of touch with ourselves that a simple government issued identification would fail to tell the story our internal capacity.

WHAT IS YOUR BRAND?

You are the brand. On the path to self-discovery you will find that your personal success must have a distinct branding that sets you apart from others. Your brand is who you are. There should not be any confusion between you and the crowd. Just as branding is a key element in the world of trade and commerce, knowing who you are is significant to your purpose in life. This is what makes you unique. It tells the world who you are, your purpose and how you influence the needs of others.

The branding of self begins at birth. A baby is full of undeveloped greatness. Your years on earth are designed to reveal the true you as you develop the product, your gift, that meets a need. A product that does not meet a need has no purpose. But before we can meet the needs of others, there must first be full development.

So how do you move beyond this robotic life of working to pay the bills and on to a path of self-discovery, success, self-actualization, and impact people for a greater change? You must first see yourself as an original; not a copy, but a true original. You are an "orig-o-pen-dinal" brand that the world has never seen before.

> *"The world in which we live is demanding new ideas, new ways of doing things, new leaders, new inventions, and new methods, styles, versions, and variations of everything...you must possess a definiteness of purpose, the knowledge of what you want and a burning desire to possess it."*
> ~Napoleon Hill

Finding the real you requires steadfastness. Over time, your values may change but your identity plays an intricate role in "self-branding." Possessing your success requires you to release your potential, and then brand yourself according to the specifications of your maker, God.

Your self-branding involves personal edification with progressive development and growth. Remember, you are a product that will be served to the world, but you must do first things first—prepare and develop. A great speaker once said real success is manifested when preparation meets opportunity. In the same way, people will remember a great product when the brand brings meaning to their lives. So, what meaning do you bring to others, and how will they remember you?

SELF-IDENTIFICATION EMANCIPATES

A major part of your journey to success greatly depends on knowing yourself better than the world knows you. *If you have no idea who you are, then you have no idea of the power that lies within you and how to manifest these internal ingredients to make them your personal reality.*

I believe the two most important questions anyone could ever ask him or herself is 'Who am I'? and 'What was I created to do'? Questions are powerful because they have a way of forcing us to focus on the important issues of life.

Could you imagine if the car did not have a purpose? Or celestial bodies like the moon, the stars and the sun had no reason to light up the heavens and provide the necessary heat to sustain life on earth? You will increase your awareness of self, your potential, and purpose as you begin to ask the right questions.

You discovered from those questions above that the natural creations, like the sun, moon and stars (celestial bodies) function correctly because they naturally know what to do. So it is with each person; the more you know about you the better you function.

TIME ALONE TO REDISCOVER

To rediscover yourself, you'll need some "alone time." If there was ever a time for you to be selfish, it is now. Breathing room is vital to self-rediscovery. You may look at it as having "me time" for you to think clearly. Getting to know yourself requires you to become your best friend.

This is the time you discover your likes and dislikes, nuances and idiosyncrasies, and then see how they gel with others. Here is where you build people skills. The way you deal with people says a lot about your personality, your brand and your product.

Unless you tell the world who you are, they will make you into whatever they wish. They will pin a tale on you and say "Giddy-up!" Take time to know you so your purpose will become evident, your brand will change lives, and your product will last.

The product of any brand is the thing that the world will consume. In this case, your product is what you give to the world, your gift. Therefore, your success is determined by how well you use your gift to influence the world around you.

THERE'S A KING INSIDE OF YOU

> *"You've forgotten who you are...never forget who you are, Simba. You are a king."*
> *~Mufasa.* (Disney movie, *The Lion King*)

Many of us have a skewed vision of who we really are. Simba, in the Disney movie, *The Lion King,* portrays this best. He was an actual king who should have been feasting on lamb chops and the most prestigious foods of the land. But when he left his kingdom for the wilderness of doubt and fear he began to feast on bugs. Imagine that...stinking bugs! What was he thinking? It's like leaving the palace for the ghetto. His only restitution then was "Hakuna Matata." Simba is not alone in this. We too allow fear, temporary circumstances and wayward teachings to dictate our actions and lead us to having false perceptions of ourselves.

I encourage you to go back (right after you finish reading this book) and watch the movie again and again until you get the real message behind the story. A memorable part in this movie is the scene when Raffiki discovered that Simba was still alive and set out to find him. Rafiki wasted no time. When he found Simba, he told him that his dad, Mufasa the king, was still alive and then led Simba through the pathway to rediscover his true nature, a reflection of the king inside of him.

Initially, Simba was in disbelief when Rafiki told him the news that his dad was alive. "Not true" he thought to himself because he witnessed the death of his dad as his uncle Scar, thrust Mufasa over the cliff and later told Simba "This is your fault, Simba. Run away, forever, and never come back!"

In the same way, we become victims of other people's circumstances. We accept their lies, develop false identities of ourselves and run away from our destiny because of fear. This is a perfect example of the type of false teachings we receive from the world, which says, run; you are not good enough; be fearful; you can't do that; why try? just give up; and stop dreaming because it's foolish.

Sometimes we forget who we are and in desperation, run to others for answers, only to find they too have no idea who you are. Most times we forget our true nature and begin to (Hakuna Matata our way through life) and happily settle for the bugs and scraps of everyday living. Who knows what you could be missing out on? Wow, just imagine! When you know who you are it will become apparent what you should not eat, and what company to keep. Until you truly discover yourself, any identity will work. However, with true self-knowledge living will become a winning process and the path you take to find personal success will be a rewarding one.

Similar to any manufacturer of a good product, the created thing is designed to manifest the thoughts and mind of the creator. A car, regardless of its make or model, will only perform to the specifications of the maker. Honda will never represent the design of BMW; neither will a tractor perform the functions of a whale. Like success, self-identification must be real.

The truth is, we've only just begun to unravel the vast complexities of the human species made in the image of God. Anything less than the real you is a waste of true potential. Do not allow your external motivations for instant gratification to become your demise. As you participate in the process of what it takes to be true to yourself in a world of make-believe, you will learn to let your discovered-self shine true for all to see.

THE TRANSFORMATION PROCESS

When you truly discover the real "YOU", you'll never wish to be anything other than the gem you've discovered in the rubble of your mind. You are like a diamond that has been under constructive pressure for many years, and at the right moment when the pressures (compression forces) reach beyond what the coal (you) can withstand, something miraculous happens, a diamond forms. You may be that diamond in its rough stages right now and yes, it is hard to see past your circumstances to behold a brighter future or see the forest for the trees, but in time you'll discover that some pressures are a necessary part of living that is purposed for your development. The only tragedy to all this is that, most of us will never become a diamond that lights up the dark world because we fear the very process that is design to transform our "coal-state" of darkness into the glistening brightness of a desirable gem.

Never despise the pressures that come to make you strong, embrace them and learn from them. You are too unique to be forgotten, and too amazing to be overlooked. You and I are souls of potentials created to do greater things than we could ever imagine. Do not hesitate to embrace the path to discover the real giant inside of you.

WELLNESS MAKES THE BRAND WORK

Another aspect of self-branding is the pursuit of "self-wellness." We should not live to get fit and healthy, we should get fit and healthy to live – better and longer.

Most people put everything before their health. This is a bad move. Part of rediscovering yourself is to identify the things that promote a healthier lifestyle. Never put anything before your health, wellness and well-being. Physical activity has a major effect on your overall well-being and it should be one of your top priorities. It changes the way you think, feel and respond to daily stimulus, good or bad.

For this reason, you are as wealthy as you are healthy, as pure as you think, and as happy as you adapt to the changes that life brings.

Directly connected to your "wealthiness" is your healthiness. They are interconnected and interdependent. *A wealthy man is a pauper without wellness and good health.* All it takes is one announcement of a terminal illness from your doctor and there goes your wealth in lieu of your health. You might have lots of money to pay for the best healthcare but it will never be enough to buy your life back.

Most people seek outer success before inner success, while others choose outer wealth over inner wellness and personal well-being. Look around, you've seen them. They are as burnt-out, frantic and stressed as a monkey with a green banana instead of a ripe one. These are people who have little or no time for anything remotely related to health and wellness, but they are the same ones screaming at their physicians, "Do something...you're a doctor, aren't you? Make me well!" They have millions in the bank of commerce, but nil in the bank of health. Like the downpour of rain on parched land so is a good wellness plan on your pathway to success.

Now, my definition of wellness may not be the same as yours or anybody else for that matter. Wellness, I believe, is everything that improves your livelihood; it is a holistic approach to a healthier lifestyle and a better way of living. Therefore, *Wellness is everything that has to do with anything you do to influence your life today for a better tomorrow.* Remember, success has little to do with your destination, but everything to do with the journey and each stop along the way.

POINTS TO PONDER

- Get to know yourself - "ALONE-TIME"
- Self-reflection brings daily revelation
- Get help when in doubt, and ask, ask, ask...
- Seek to build quality relationships
- Team up with others who are doing good
- Develop a healthy habit of visiting your doctor
- Take in adequate amounts of water daily
- Participate in ongoing fitness activities
- Reduce the amount of time you spend sitting
- Move to win, or sit to lose...you choose

CHAPTER THREE

GET LIVING
YOUR BEST – ANYWAY

"Dreams will cause you to leave your zone of comfort in order to realize the true meaning of living life to its fullest."
~Andrew E. Guy

NOTES

DO IT ANYWAY...

People are often unreasonable, illogical, and self-centered; forgive them anyway.

If you are kind, people may accuse you of selfish, ulterior motives; Be kind anyway.

If you are successful, you will win some false friends and some true enemies; Succeed anyway.

If you are honest and sincere, people may cheat you; Be honest and sincere anyway.

If you find serenity and happiness, they may be jealous; Be happy anyway.

The good you do today, people will often forget tomorrow; Do good anyway.

Give the world the best you have, and it may never be enough; Give the world the best you've got anyway.

You see, in the final analysis, it is between you and God; It was never between you and them anyway.

— This version credited to Mother Teresa

As you Work Your Words and decide to give living your best shot there will be "haters" along the way. Unlike the people in your corner who truly desire your success, "haters" despise you for wanting success, and like misery, they too, love company. Acknowledge them, work your words and keep it moving. Do not stop for them. *If they are not in it to help you win it, they are there to see you lose it.* Use them as fuel to push you in the right direction—forward, up, and beyond. As you will discover, working the right words and the motion of forward-thinking is lotion for your pathway to success, it makes the journey smoother.

Doing it anyway empowers you to be focus on the things that you speak and set out to do. Regardless of your situation or circumstances, all things are possible if you'd only believe. (I know you've heard that phrase a million times now, but I'll say it again and again, and as often as I need to repeat it so it sinks deep into your consciousness.) And when you believe it, you'll do what it says.

Remember among words diligently worked, decisions reign supreme on the hierarchical scale of success, and people will talk the moment you decide to activate your spoken words to pursue your goals and dreams. Do not let this hamper your groove. People will talk about you whether you fail or succeed. This is a fact of living. Keep moving and just-do-it-anyway, "Just-DIA". It doesn't matter your ethnicity, be it black or white, red-necked, country or city folk, Indian, Chinese, Jew or gentile; "Just-DIA". Give them something to talk about. Now, don't you stop there; go as far as making it impossible for them to forget about you as well.

Everywhere they look, they should see you, hear you, and even want to shake your hand. In their living rooms on their television sets (providing they have one), you should be there; in the newspapers (providing they can read) you should be there; on billboards (providing they can see), you should be there; on their radios (providing they can hear), you should be there; and everywhere they mention good news, you should be there. Be there anyway, "Just-BTA."

And why not? Believe me, you were made for this. Like Esther in the bible, who become a beacon of light and the vessel through which her people were saved from annihilation, you were made for such a time as this. I say "Just-DIA".

Success is like glue, it attracts every walk-of-life toward you as you begin to work your words. This happens the moment you decide to dream, believe and step out of the proverbial "box-thinking" way of existing, and make your reality worth living. The personal freedom of success releases you from the clutches of people, the snares of pessimistic naysayers and the dream-killing on-looking bystanders. Trust me, they will be there, but "Just-DIA". Stop being a spectator of life. It's your turn at bat, step up and take a swing at living and give the world something spectacular to catch!

THE PATH OF HINDRANCE

Unless you do something you've never done before, you'll never accomplish your dreams nor work the words you speak. One thing is certain; humans have different levels of fear intolerance, and the mental consciousness to conquer them. Fear is a crippling force that stops us dead in our tracks. In other words, fear can also be any debilitating force that stops you from moving forward, overcoming setbacks, and breaking through to victory. Zig Ziglar says, "Fear is **f**alse **e**vidence **a**ppearing **r**eal" and most of what we fear is mental, but when placed into its right perspective we can all agree that our fear factors are not all that monstrous when we take the first step to conquer them.

In order for you to give life your best shot you must face your fears to overcome them. Taking on the challenges will provide you with the experience you need to face other fears and win.

Tangible experience plays an important role; they are priceless, and they provide significant learning opportunities for growth. You must also think of big fears as a bunch of little fears culminating as one. Therefore, it is to your advantage that you conquer your little fears quickly. Never wait for tomorrow to do what you must do today. You stand to gain more from living when you have the experiences to make informed decisions. Therefore, to overcome your fear you must attack it head-on. You are what you think, but you become what you do, an overcomer.

THE PATH OF PERSEVERANCE

> *"It is never the things we acquire throughout life...(that matters), but rather, it is the person we become."*
> ~ Less Brown

Take what life gives you and make it into what you want. Don't give up, but "give-in" to what you are called to do. Giving your best shot requires tenacity, determination, vigor and "with-it-ness." In case you are wondering what I mean by the term "with-it-ness" it is an ability to be cognizant of your surroundings and the sequences of events as they occur. You know, live in the moment. Be there, not in a few years; be there now.

To give living your best shot, you must be willing to try harder than you are willing to quit. The moment you refuse to try is the day you announce your death sentence to the world. Be strong. Take courage, and keep your chin up, because life is a gift, but living is process that begins and ends with a fight of faith.

Remember, for everything you can imagine there's a pathway with your name on it and it has an ultimate design called success. Your greatest challenge will be people. You must be agile, flexible adaptable, and possess a high level of social skills to be successful. You must be ready and willing to make the necessary changes to overcome obstacles. Seek out opportunities of growth, and self-improvement.

MANAGE YOURSELF
BUT MEASURE YOUR TIME

After you've rediscovered yourself, branded, developed and "overstood" your purpose, you are now ready to serve your gift to the world. On this path, all streets lead to success and every highway and bridge is named after you—and they all say in unison "Go...Go...Go! But what if they don't say go? What will you do? Will you quit or keep moving forwards?

I say keep it moving, and give it your best shot. This is your moment and this is your time. You'll find that most people are hard workers, who diligently pursue success. But the sad thing is that they do not know when it is their time. It's important you understand timing and to use it effectively to measure your progress to success. It allows you to convert your previous efforts into a harvest of hope.

As a young boy growing up in the foothills of the Caribbean in Jamaica, West Indies, I've always heard a saying which went like this: "Time is the master." Since then, it has taken me some years to come to grips with this saying. It was not until recently that I came to the realization that time is not my master. It is however, a measure of how I spend each moment on earth. So there you have it, time is only a measure, not your master!

SUCCESS THROUGH OUTREACH

> *"One hand washes the other
> and they both get cleaned"*
> -Andrew E. Guy

To give life your best shot you'll need the right people who want you to succeed. Remember success is both personal and public. Working your words and Personal development is the private side, while people are the public aspect of your success. People generate creativity and innovations. You will need effective people skills to help you navigate your way to personal success. You may not always know everyone you meet; some can be complete strangers, while others may enter your pathway for only a season. Despite the length of the season, you should always find pathways to use your gift to reach people.

There are many ways you can use your gift to help others. Think of outreach as "stepping-out" of your zone of comfort to share your gift to the world. I encourage you to seek out ways to make a difference in people's life. Contact your local youth organizations, church groups and other non-profit organizations in your community. Another way to serve is through mentorship, volunteering to assist with afterschool tutoring, join a community sport team to assist with coaching.

SUCCESS THROUGH RELATIONSHIPS

Remember, *things never change until you do—and a vision never dies—only people without one do.* Begin by developing relationships with people who honestly care about you and are motivated to see you succeed. Most times you'll find that you making it mean more to them than the very words they use to motivate you. Having the right people in your corner is like having the key to a treasure chest.

They will help you gain access to new opportunities, open doors, and are there to give you constructive feedback imperative to your advancement. They will tell you the truth regardless of the temporary pain you feel. They will not sugarcoat the facts, especially when it comes to your growth.

BRAND YOUR SUCCESS WITH HIGH STANDARDS

You should always make honesty, integrity and accountability the standards that guide your success. This is not an overnight ordeal, and these things are never easy to do because there will always be the temptation to compromise. It takes commitment, hard work, and dedication. But the success of your brand will become more established as you maintain your standard.

> *"The purpose of the product is found only in the mind of the creator"*
> (Myles Munroe).

POINTS TO PONDER

Never wait for tomorrow to do what you must do today. The gap to self-discovery has increased significantly, and has been widened to guesswork and assumptions.

Think of it this way. A man once believed he was a giant in all the land because of his stature, physical outlook and prized possessions. At the end of his time, he was saddened on his deathbed when he came to realize that while life was his gift, the process of living was his ultimate opportunity to use his gift to change the world.

He did everything he possibly could, and for the wrong reasons; the eye-pleasing pleasure of his many adoring fans who thought he had everything and they too, wanted to be like him. At the end of your life, nothing else matters; not your belongings, possessions, who knows you, nor what you've discovered from the many books you've read. They mean absolutely nothing; so, open the gift of life, and allow the process of living to reveal your giftedness to the world.

CHAPTER FOUR

DARE TO DREAM

"Dreams will cause you to leave your zone of comfort in order to realize the true meaning of living life to its fullest."
~Andrew E. Guy

NOTES

_____

The desire to live life to its fullest demands that you dream big. As I said before, BIG dreaming is a personality of success. This is the initial step in working your words. You see, once you begin thinking about possibilities for a better life you have already begun to speak – internally. The next step is to speak those dreams aloud to yourself first (even in the mirror), then to a few trusted people. After this you launch out and work those words, utilizing all the resources available to you (including this book, of course).

Dreams are not just the personality of success, they are a substance of life and nourishment for living. What could one dream do? Free an oppressed race of people, provide wells for people in remote regions to get clean water, simplify computer processing so that a larger population of the world can own computers and even lead a young man from a single parent home to become the first black President of the United States. On a more personal note, it was a dream that led my mother to embark on a journey to leave Jamaica and work hard in Canada so that her six children could join her and have a better life as well.

From Dr. Martin Luther King Jr. to the late Nelson R. Mandela, to Mother Teresa, and countless others, including those whose work went by unnoticed, have given their lives for the betterment of mankind and the world at large. It was because of their dreams that we enjoy better lives today. So never look at dreaming as a waste of time – that only happens if you never act on it. I urge you, dare to dream!

B.I.G. DREAMS – A STORY

I am reminded of a story about a young man who made dreaming his way of living and a method to transforming his life. One day as he sat down next to a pond he had a dream. Let's read his account of what happened...

I remember quite vividly one foggy Monday morning my little brother and I sat down beside the old pond.

Everything that you could possibly dream of happened there. This pond was filled with many different creatures - snails, snakes, fishes, and frogs; trust me, if you could name them, they were there in that old pond.

Unlike other mornings, this one was very unusual. It was quiet. In fact, the moment was ripe for dreaming! Aside from my little brother's nose that was always running like a sewer in

Manhattan, I had other things on my mind. As we sat there beneath the withered grapefruit tree, next to the old pond with my feet taking a religious bath in the chilly morning water, I had the dream of a lifetime!

I have always been the type of person who knew there was something special for everyone, including little me. You know, doing something B.I.G! **Bold, Intuitive** *and* **Gutsy!** *That's right, doing something so big it gave new meaning to the word itself* **(Bold-Intuitive-Gutsy)***. In fact, I dreamt so much I often thought of myself as Joseph the "dreamer" from the bible story. You remember the one whose brothers hated him because he was highly favored by his father? And one time he had a weird dream about being a great ruler, his brothers bowing down to him, and to make things worse he even had a coat of many colors that was given to him by his father, Jacob. Good ole "Joe-Joe" the dreamer, who became a great ruler in Egypt and was even used by God to save his entire family.*

Oh yeah, about my dream...

So there I was in New York City, the 'Big Apple' that never sleeps and where a moment of silence seems almost impossible to be wished upon, like a star that never shines. Crazy huh? But anyway here's my story...

It was late one Saturday night when I received the call to perform live at 'Showtime at the Apollo.' By the way, the Apollo is one of the greatest stages known to performers worldwide. Moreover, this stage has made kings of those who dared to dream and who had the "B.I.G" courage to grace the worn out floors of its stage.

Since the opening of the theater, dreams have taken on the shape of wings and soared. As a young boy, I once heard that this stage was so "LUGE" (too large to be big and too huge to be large). It had both upper and lower balconies along with a stage so grand I could play a full nine innings of baseball with the great-famed-slugger himself—Babe Ruth. On a given night, I imagined this Titanic could hold close to ten thousand people, a crowd so "luge" that, upon applause could crack a hole in the back windshield of a 1950 Jimmy Blazer. Bang! And there it goes— shattered to smithereens!—A force so strong and everlasting that among the many newscasters, CNN would spend eternity trying to put the pieces back together in their "Special Reports".

Anyway, this place was fruitful and full of substance. As a matter of fact, it almost seemed as if anyone who had the guts to step "soles" on that stage could make his-story! Whoa! Me performing on the 'BIG' stage; what a Bold, Intuitive and Gutsy courageous move. I know mom and dad would've been proud to see me; I just know they would. But still, I'm only dreaming...or am I?

As the late evening drew closer to midnight, I made my way through the bustling New York City traffic. When I arrived at the Apollo in Harlem, my palms began to sweat like a puppy dog's nose. The bumpy bus ride crushed my clothes like unwanted autumn leaves on the back of a city garbage truck at rush hour on a busy Friday. And the constant rubbing of other passengers from the packed vehicle had me smelling like rotten eggs; Smell-eee! You know the type. I was tired and flustered from the long, aggravating ride on the New York City Transit System, simply worn out, if you asked me.

*Suddenly, the dream wasn't so dreamy anymore; and like Joseph, I felt as if I were in a cave waiting for some passerby to place their highest bids and cast lots for the my "techni-colored" coat. The Apollo didn't seem so glamorous anymore. I wanted to go home! At least then I could be in my warm bed, smelling fresh from my recent hot shower and kicking back in my comfy pajamas watching my favorite movie **'Glory'** for the nine millionth time. Something about that Morgan*

Freeman guy...he's a great actor...anyway let's continue.

In any case, I did reach my destination. All of a sudden, the place seemed strange, as if I were in another world. There were people everywhere, enjoying themselves and waiting for the show. I made my way to a back door entrance and allowed myself in. There I waited for about two minutes and then the show coordinator came back stage and offered me a suit of clothes to change into and a cup of hot tea, which I was desperately craving.

Soon it would be my turn to take the stage and follow in the footsteps of former greats like Bill Cosby, Eddie Murphy, Richard Pryor, and the likes. In many ways, this made me feel very humble and a little childish, yet eager to please the fans who took the time to come out on a cold winter's night to be warmed by humor that surpasses mere dreaming of the good 'ole days.

For a moment, it was almost unreal! Imagine me: that 'ole diamond in the ruff, LIVE at THE APOLLO - whoa! Dreams were meant for moments like these, breath taking!

The thought of it troubled me happily and kept my feet busy. Moments before my name was announced, I started my usual get-ready routine, pacing back and forth continuously.

Finally, it was my time to perform. Yeah, the 'Big Apple!' I wondered what one dream could do. First, the curtain went up, the spotlight switched on; and then suddenly, there was a charge in the air. At this time, the seats were jam packed with comedy fans anxiously waiting to be joked out of their paid spots by this rising star.

My heart pounded vigorously in the cavity of my chest; man, it was racing! Vroom, vroom, like the fastest car in the Indianapolis 500.

Although I could hardly see their faces due to the darkness and the bright overpowering lights, I could feel what felt like hundreds of eyes looking at me all at once.

The stage lights slowly undimmed, and a touch of the microphone sent sudden chills down my spine. My mouth began to spring water, like an overused brush at an all-night car wash. Next, I heard what sounded like the shuffling of feet and the screeching of seats and chairs as fans drew closer toward the edge of their seats to hear my opening act.

Meanwhile, the sound coordinator made final adjustments to the audio system to ensure my microphone was perfectly tuned. This was as intense as it could get for me. I felt every bit of emotion that any human could have ever felt. And if words would permit me, I would bottle up every smidgen of wired anatomically neurological sensation that ran through my body—from brain to neuron, and from cell body to axon, to dendrite, to synapse to innervation and back.

Boy, that is a mouthful...Whew! But, hey, I'm only dreaming...

So there I was, in the heat of the moment, and Bang! My first joke knocked the roof of the building like a strong wind having a tug of war with a grown man's toupee on the Trump tower...zing...gone. And then I heard what sounded like an ocean wave of laughter rippling through the audience. Crowds of people were laughing, cheering, whistling and screaming for more. Could you believe it? I know I can; in fact, I am now a firm believer about doing it "B.I.G."

Joy came with great sigh of long awaiting relief. This was the best opener I had ever done! Mind you, I'm still dreaming, so you may just have to pinch me so I can continue to enjoy this moment before I either pass out or the moment passes me by. But under no circumstances will I allow that to happen. I am hanging on to this moment for dear life like my future and the sanity of my soul depends on it.

A few moments later I thought to myself. Why on God's green earth was I so nervous to begin with. Then it dawned on me; the answer came to me like a renaissance. I'm a star with a great light inside me that must shine in a dark world that is full of hate, and greed, lust and sin, and people who are hurting, lonely, forgotten, weak and in desperate need of help. It was at that moment when I realized that I am a gift to the world, sent here miles away from the mind of a creative creator, into the heart of the world and from a stinky old pond, to put a smile on people's faces.

And regardless of your dreaming place, be it in a secluded room, behind the wheel of your jalopy or "Benzo," or like me beside a stinky old pond with my runny-nose brother—let dreams reign in your soul! Dare to dream....

POINTS TO PONDER

Regardless of your state in life, there's greatness inside of you. Don't go to the grave with it, for this would be your greatest tragedy: taking with you to your grave something that was meant to be left behind for the world to experience.

A great speaker once said that the graveyard is the wealthiest place on earth. Why? Because so much that was meant to be accomplished and given to the world was hidden, kept and buried forever in the grave. Therefore, I say the world would be an even greater place if it could find a way to resurrect buried gifts and transfer them to those who are willing to manifest them to benefit humanity.

Remember to shine your light, which is your product and gift to the world, so that great men may see your good works as you work your words and give glory to your creator, God. However, in order to light up this dark world, you must dream "B.I.G!" For there are no small dreams where you came from, and it gets even bigger where you are going. And make it your goal to take others along with you in order for them to experience their B.I.G dreams too.

There are millions of people in the world today who forfeited their dreams for a better future only to settle for the scraps of today. No one knows for sure why people continue to do it. Perhaps it is because they cannot see it through or because they cannot see through the clouds of negativity, shortcomings, struggles, hard times, disappointments, ridicule and loneliness. Or perhaps it is because the dreams seemed much bigger than they thought they could handle, so they become overwhelmed and discard them. Irrespective of the reasons, you don't have to be a follower; become a pioneer. Blaze the path for others and lead the way. Put action to your dreams and work your words.

Today hundred, thousands, millions if not, billions of people, live in despair and anger over dreams they failed to see through the end. This my friends, is the greatest tragedy of wasted years.

Do not live with regret, wondering what could have happened if you had at least tried; what difference could you have made if you did not stand behind fear, shame and become daunted by the view that dreaming is only for the ones who are coo-coo, nuts, "co-razy," and "fairytale-minded." Make sure your dreams are bigger than you are so that it will take you a lifetime to give it away to the world.

CHAPTER FIVE

MIND-SET MATTERS

"Before a man can accomplish anything of any enduring nature in the world, he must first of all acquire some measure of success in the management of his own mind."
~James Allen

NOTES

For any Success-driven activity to become a reality it must first begin with the end in mind. In the field of education we call it *understanding by design*; this is where you plan your lessons based on the objectives you expect your students to accomplish, beginning with the end in mind. For you personally, this means you must have a picture (which may not always be clear at first, but is vital) of the final product you want to end up with. What do you see when you are by yourself and all your friends are gone? Do you see greatness, success, triumph, and determination? If not, you are looking at the wrong picture and you need to construct a new image.

One of the most important characteristics of successful people is that they speak what they want, then follow-up with progressive-minded action that produces lasting results. Therefore, what you say to yourself is far more important to your personal development than all the advice or accolades people could ever give you. They could put your name in lights, on Broadway or on the Hollywood Walk of Fame; but if your success is not embedded deep within your psyche, with a strong foundation that is unwavering, and unshakeable, you are simply a temporary fad that is here today and gone tomorrow. Don't get me wrong, external feedback is good; they do play a role and they do have a place in the grand scheme of things, but your world is created inside out, not the reverse.

THINK BIGGER

Your mind is the fertile ground where every productive thought is generated. You can actually think your way to success, but you must first become the mental creator of your own success. The bottom line is that you will have no staying power if you fail to think. Mind power is the most powerful force on planet earth; not bombs or weapons of warfare and mass destruction - but the mind. As such, a success-minded approach is the exchange of your small thinking for something bigger.

If your biggest dreams can be accomplished in only five to ten years you haven't yet begun to dream. Your dreams should be over the span of a lifetime; and in some cases, your dream should be so big that it will become an inheritance for your children's, children. There are no small dreams in the minds of success-driven individuals. This happens because they choose to think longer, bigger and more tenaciously than most. You must engage your mind in productive thinking daily. It is often said that you are the product of your environment, but even more, I believe you are both the raw material and the product of your thinking. Mindset matters; **you are what you think but you become what you practice.** Your actions are a result of your thinking. In the words of Bruce Lee, *"Knowledge is not enough, one must apply...willingness is not enough, one must do."*

Your world is created by your thinking, and there is absolutely nothing you cannot achieve if you put your mind to it. However, there will be difficult times, but these are part of the process of shaping you into a masterpiece of resiliency. There will be mountains to climb and hurdles to jump, but your mind is stronger than any obstacles you will ever face. You are a product of a supernatural creative God, who has made you a replica (copy) of himself. He has placed inside you the ability to think beyond your greatest expectations. But in order to achieve the invisible you must think beyond the visible that you see. The great physicist, Albert Einstein, once said, *"The world that we've created is a product of our thinking; it cannot be changed without changing our thinking; therefore, we are the product of our thinking."*

I have come to this revelation that there are no little and big people in the world; never was, neither will there ever be. What we do have are a lot of little stinkers and a few big thinkers. Little stinkers are small thinkers, people who have become so close to their own fears that the mere smell of it makes them regurgitate every bit of confidence they needed to take the first step of faith to make their dreams come true.

OVERCOMING FAILURE-CONSCIOUSNESS

Some people are more fear-conscious and failure-intuitive than they are success-minded. Because of this mindset, many do not see success as part of their lives, neither can they imagine it happening to them at all. They are sedentary in their thinking and therefore, require someone to wheel them around the maze of reality as they dream a new snore.

Wake up! Don't let this mindset be in you. This is a failure-conscious mindset that never leads to victorious living. Having a poor mindset will cripple your chances to succeed at anything in life, leaving you paralyzed with little hopes of ever stepping out of your comfort zone to take on the challenges of living. It's a battle out there but you are more than equipped to eliminate the battlefield in your mind.

THINK FREE

Even though mental slavery can be a stumbling block, freedom is only a thought away. I am reminded of the movie *ShawShank Redemption*, with Tim Robins starring as Andy Dufresne. Here is a banker who committed a crime and was confined as a prisoner to a jail cell. He chose to think his way out of the grime and filth and onto an oceanfront of destiny as he prepared is dream boat.

Despite the warden's mistreatment and ill-use of his talents, Dufresne used his mind to plan one of the greatest escapes known to convicts. The warden was completely stunned and flabbergasted. In fact, it got so overwhelming that he killed himself. Dufresne used the power of his mind to get the best of him.

While he was in prison, he used his gift of financial expertise to set up bank accounts on the outside using the warden's ill-gotten funds. Dufresne even went as far as doing taxes for the jail staff and got the warden to provide ice-cold beers for the other prisoners as they resurfaced the prison roofs.

And he did not stop there; Andy Dufresne reopened the prison library, ordered hundreds of books, taught other prisoners how to read and coached them to complete their first high school diplomas; all of this without them ever stepping foot into a classroom. Some even went on to complete college degrees while they were locked up and confined to a jail cell. Imagine that. You have no excuse because you are free with no prison cells to enclose you except those inside your mind.

ACTIVATE THE RIGHT MINDSET

The right mindset doesn't just appear out of thin air; it must be activated, watered with the right material, and nourished. In order to find your pathway to personal success, you must embrace change, think big, and with great hopes, talk about the tomorrows that you've never seen or felt, but only imagined. It is a new mindset that you have to embrace. All obstacles were designed with a purpose in mind, to make you stronger than the task ahead requires. And the faster you overcome your challenges, the quicker destiny is actualized.

Look at it this way, a fearful-mindset is like an unforgiving mindset. It takes more energy to hold on to unforgiveness than it does to forgive others. In fact, fear and unforgiveness are so toxic that they can kill you. Mind you, the same amount of energy it takes to think negatively is the same amount of energy it would take to think positively and constructively. And you can do all of this faster than you could say, "Switch!"

Now, don't get me wrong when I use the words, fast or quick; there's no rat race in success. Time is the measurement by which we progress through the stages of living, but it is only an indication of how long you spent doing what has occupied your conscious mind.

I have said this before, there is no such thing as time management. It does not exist, as far as your personal success is concerned. You can have success now if you so choose; you just have to start thinking about it. And no, this statement is neither contradicting nor confounding. You cannot control time; you can only control yourself.

Self-control, believe it or not, begins in the mind. Your thoughts provide the rationale or reasoning that guides your active, and in many ways, your passive behaviors. Bad things can and will happen but countering them with the right thoughts will catapult you forward to personal success. Right thinking will always lead to good things, even in the midst of chaos. Begin this journey today. Think right and right will happen. Do not wait. Begin now, your future is riding on it.

> *"Through imagination, we can visualize the uncreated worlds of potential that lie within us....therefore; I can live out my imaginations instead of my memories."*
> ~Stephen R. Covey

As you think, so you will live. Thinking therefore, is how we experience the world around us. Within this realm of thinking, we learn to love, hate, fear, and to be brave; to let go and move on or to hold on to yesterday's hurts and failures in lieu of the successes of tomorrow. It is often said that "a mind is a terrible thing to waste," and it really is.

There are many other sayings and clichés that have become ineffective and overused. But the value of the saying "Mind over Matter" still prevails. You see, your mindset matters because it is the only enabler or immobilizer that supersedes our reality. We are able to overcome challenges despite what reality throws at us, but our rate of survival is often determined by our thinking. I believe this is a process of thinking that is designed to elevate us from a state of mediocrity to a state of excellence that reflects the very essence of God himself.

THE RIGHT SUBSTANCE

Ideas are golden but your experiences are treasures. When the experiences are applied through right thinking you will overcome obstacles put in your pathway.

Thoughts are like the forces of nature, always present. While the moon may be 153 million miles away from earth, it still possesses the ability to affect the ocean tides. But unlike the vast distance of the moon from the earth, our ever-present thoughts transform our lives daily.

There is no distance in thought; the only physical manifestation is procrastination. In the words of Napoleon Hill, "One idea is all you need to achieve personal success." However, let me hastened to add, that this might be one of ten thousand other ideas that you've tried. The point is, do not be afraid of unsuccessful attempts, for out of these can come your "golden-egg". Remember Thomas Edison, the inventor of the light bulb? His golden-idea illuminated after about five thousand experiments! In the same light, be mindful what you think, and be conscious of the thoughts that shape your present and future worlds; for therein lies the key to open the unseen doors of living. Be an original.

MOVE BEYOND CIRCUMSTANCES

> *"Intentions will always override expectation where your mindset matters."*
> *~Andrew E. Guy*

Circumstances will change, but mindset is the determining factor that gives you wings to fly above the impossibilities of living. It is vital that you see life as a gift, and living as a process. The two are interdependent, but completely different. There is nothing you could do about the family you're born to, the time you took your first breath, and the doctor that first slapped you on the buttocks and made you cry as you searched for oxygen. However, the pathways you take are the complete opposite. You choose. Therefore, living is the process by which you open your life (the gift), explore and develop it and then give it to the world as a product of your brand, the real you.

In the novel, *Who Moved My Cheese*, the author, Dr. Spencer Johnson, used two mice (Sniff and Scurry) to demonstrate how having the right mindset can prepare us for unforeseen changes. They had a proactive mindset that propelled them to expand both their thinking and their boundaries. This is a trait of B.I.G. thinking. Take the limits off perceived limitations and move beyond what is expected to what is intended, success.

You'll find people's expectations can be a capped ceiling that hinders you from finding your pathway to personal success. Again, *your success is not out-there, "it is in-there."* It is not based on the praises of others because true success is a personal freedom that becomes activated when you use your words to shape your world. The difference between you and others is that people have expectations of what they think you should or should not do. I call these "success-limitations." The opposite is true; their expectations are not your intentions, and the truth is, they will never be. Therefore, intentions will always override expectation; and this is where your mindset matters.

Sniff and Scurry's names are significant to their purpose. In life, you have to 'sniff' out new grounds, new opportunities, new beginnings and forget old experiences at times. Your priorities will change but the real you should not; you are still the value associated with your brand. Then after you've sniffed out the new pathways to your personal success, you'll need to 'scurry' (hasten) your way to make these new opportunities your reality.

Dr. Johnson's novel, *Who Moved My Cheese*, also included two 'little people' or humans, called Hem and Haw. Unlike the mice, the humans who lived in the maze got so comfortable with their lifestyle, that even when the food ran out, one of them preferred to stay and starve rather than seek out food for his survival. This story of mice versus humans really shows how slow the latter can be to adapting to change. The human response was so slow that it almost led to their extinction!

Like most people, little stinkers and small thinkers are oblivious to life-changing opportunities. But there are some opportunities we cannot afford to miss. These are crucially timed-moments that arise throughout the process of living that bridges the gaps to create the pathways to your true destiny. All meaningful opportunities are seized by faith. So, in addition to having the right mindset, you must believe you can.

THE LEAP OF FAITH

I think that some movies are forces of momentum that push our boundaries of comfort. Some give us a glimpse of the future while others leave an indelible imprint that either transforms us or leaves us confounded. I am not a movie fan in the least but there are a few movies that I consider timeless classics for the lessons they teach us about living. Among these few 'classics' my favorite of all times is Indiana Jones and the Last Crusade, starring Sir Sean Connery and Harrison Ford.

There was a powerful scene in which Ford, in his quest for the Holy Grail and to save Connery's life, had to cross a bottomless canyon, and the only way to do this was by taking a personal leap of faith. This scene is called the *'Leap of faith'* for that very reason. Most times our leap of faith becomes the necessity to save the lives of others. The same is true for everyone in life. We all have specific pathways that we must travel, which requires a leap of faith to find personal success. Knowing that your personal success may be the lifesaver for others should be a valid reason for you to step out of comfort zone and into your destiny.

Indiana Jones tried everything in his power to make that leap of faith to cross over, but nothing worked. In his desperation, he pulled out his little pocket book with the map and the instructions to the Grail. At the same time the camera flashes back to Connery, who gasped at his last breath to say, "You Must Believe, Boy; You Must Believe!" The camera then switches back to Indy as he clenched his bare chest, lifted his right leg clad in a dusty, worn-out shoe, closed his eyes and then took the step of faith into the abyss.

Suddenly, the ground came to meet his foot and he was shocked to find himself standing in the presence of the valley of death. It was breathtaking! After the path became visible to him, Indy used some gravel to mark the trail for others to see. This is why it is vital that you have the right mindset, discover yourself, know that you are the brand, and that your gift is the product by which you influence the lives of people and change your world.

Ford's character, Indiana Jones or Indy, is a representation of us traveling on our specific roads to self-discovery. The interesting thing is that the success of others is contingent upon the goals we achieve for ourselves. These people could be your family members, co-workers, the stranger on the streets, or that bum on the corner begging for food. Our goals may be personal at first but they will have a public impact. Therefore, you must believe you have the right mindset to work your words into reality even when the path seems invisible. Remember, the journey of a million miles begins with the first step.

BELIEVE TO ACHIEVE

Do you believe? If so, in what? As crazy as this may sound, many people equate FAITH and BELIEF as aspects of religion. This is as far from the truth as the assertion that humans are derived from monkeys. There is no living without believing. You see, every person on planet earth believes and has faith in something, someone, or some ultimate power. It takes faith to accomplish anything in life. Even the very process of life is an act of faith, unless we tamper with the master design and call it science.

Living is meaningless without faith and belief. Faith is a state of mind, while believing is a function that produces action. Look around, everything your senses reveal to you (science and technology, advanced innovations, works of art, and enchanting musical composition) are all a result of faith and belief. These and other such acts are only possible as a result of faith and belief. Your success is no accident and neither are you different from those who have come and gone before. If they can do it, by faith, so can you.

You must be alert and discern the times. Moments are never identical; they may look similar, but they are never the same. Success comes in many forms but personal success is paramount of all and you must be prepared. A speaker once said success happens when preparation meets opportunity. Indeed, but what does that say about us? Remember, opportunities have a shelf life; they do not linger forever. Therefore, you must seize them in their lifetime while you can.

Like success, I believe many people have the wrong concept of destiny; this is why some never find it. Most believe it is some mythical fate that appears in the future, somewhere. On the contrary, I believe your destiny is now, today, and doing what you were created to do; not some "futuristic-tomorrows" that may never come. Destiny is like a door waiting, everyone who dares to enter can knock, open it, let go of doubts and explore the world. So what is this destiny we humans seek so desperately? Is it tangible? Can you touch it, smell it, see and behold it? Yes; destiny is a state of total freedom where the optimal functioning of an individual becomes possible and the mind is free of doubt. In the presence of mental freedom, nothing is impossible. Your destiny is having a mindset that empowers you to apply your gifts and freely use them to meet the needs of the world. It is what you were created to experience, and your reason for living is to help others to find their pathway to reach their destiny too.

LIVE THE DREAM

Adopting the mindset of great dreamers will cause you to replicate their success; moreover, your goal is not just to repeat their actions of success but to improve and supersede them. Dr. Martin Luther King Jr. once said, "I have a dream. I have seen the promise land...I may not get there with you, but...." I am therefore convinced that our goal is no longer to have dreams, but to live the dreams that Dr. King Jr. had for us. To be judged by the content of your character and not by the color of your skin, and to have equal access to resources that improve the livelihood of all. This was his dream. Stop dreaming, now is the time to live them. Are you living the dream our repeating "history"? It is full time for you to live and rewrite "your-story" instead of reliving history.

To reach your destiny you must be willing to let go of what you have to get what you want; but even better, to get what you were created to achieve in this life, not some distant future. Even though destiny is present, most people miss it because it requires B.I.G. thinking. Small thinkers often miss their destiny. Let go, and let growth take you places.

The reality of small thinking is fear that results in death. Your pathway to personal success is worth discovering but you must have the right mindset and willingness to grow. Mindset matters most where effective living is concerned.

Big thinkers on the other hand are "globalistic" and optimistic in their thinking. These people believe in the impossible—they are the faithful and committed. These are the "I-will overcome"—even if it means the end of me. Their view of reality adjusts as opportunities of growth and expansion is envisioned. Big thinkers are regular people with Big thoughts, Big hearts and Big imaginations that are contagiously inspirational and their gift (the product) is used as a tool of empowerment that changes the world for good. Are you doing this with your life?

POINTS TO PONDER

- Become a BIG thinker: Big thinkers are regular people with Big thoughts, Big hearts and BIG imaginations
- Think your way outside the makeshift boxed-in mindset
- imaginations that are contagiously inspirational and their gift (the product) is used as a tool of empowerment that changes the world for good.
- It takes faith to accomplish anything in life.
- The reality of small thinking is fear that results in death.
- Don't just have dreams, live the dreams of the BIG dreamer before you

CHAPTER SIX

WORDS THAT W.O.R.K. TO MOTIVATE

*"Changing your thinking, changes your words,
and right speaking changes your way of living."*
~Andrew E. Guy

NOTES
_____

You really do not need a PhD to change your life, just have the desire to make change happen. Sometimes living may weigh you down and unforeseen obstacles may lead to unaccomplished tasks, seemingly setting you back on your mental success course. Be encouraged and do not lose sight of your goals. They may not come when you want them, but they will be there when you need them the most, at the right time. This too is part of the process of living. While you may not need a PhD to change your life, you'll definitely need to have the function of a PHD to acquire the guts to overcome tough times, to work your words, and to find your pathway of success.

Some people have doubts and resort to fearful tactics to deal with change. Doubt is like a cancer to the body. Cancer disrupts vital functions and weakens the body's immune system rendering it vulnerable to external viral attacks. Like the body, when you have doubt you too become internally weak, vulnerable and dependent on external support, this impedes your motivation to succeed.

However, this approach has an adverse effect on the individual. According to Napoleon Hill, "Change is a builder and not a destroyer; it is the beginning of new things and not the ending of life." In addition, change has a built-in mechanism that improves and sustains those who embrace it.

So what did I mean when I said you don't need a PhD but you actually do need the function of a PHD to make your dreams come true? Well, the function of a PHD in this sense is an acronym for what I call, *"Past Having Doubts."*

PAST HAVING DOUBTS

How do you get past having doubts to move into victorious living? This is not an easy task but it is possible to become a PHD and doubt free. It means looking at yourself in a different light, far beyond what you normally think. PHD requires letting go of who you are to become what you should be. It means adopting a positive forward-thinking mindset and a heart of forgiveness. Most people have a tough time forgiving themselves and others for life's disappointments. Let it go and free yourself.

Mistakes will happen, plans will fail, and things do fall apart at times, but you should never give up on your dreams. Remember, if you dream B.I.G. enough, all you need is one dream to come true and it will dramatically change your life. Do not allow your disappointments to define who you are, but be defined by your true self. Learn from your setbacks and used them as fuel to propel you further along your pathway to your destiny.

Let's be honest here, there will be moments in your life that rock your foundation to its core. But as ludicrous as this may sound, these are the greatest moments of living. ***It will take the better of you to get the best out of you.*** Nevertheless, don't quit...keep your mind on the prize.

BECOMING LABEL-FREE

The world has made it impossible to function without labels. As part of a built-in safety mechanism, every product and chemical is mandated to have some form of safety labels affixed to it in order to protect the user and the public. This need for labeling has become the cornerstone to providing safety information in the industrialized world known as the MSDS (Material Safety Data Sheet). The MSDS is a legal document containing information on the potential side effects to your health from exposure to certain chemicals. Labels not only serve as safety warnings but they tell users the purpose and potential health side effects of the chemical, and how to use them safely.

Unlike products and dangerous chemicals, humans were created label-free but over time we become the unintended product of societal labeling: "Failure", "Loser", and "Underachiever", just to name a few. It appears that even though we were created label-free, mankind has chosen to take on the functions of the labels others have placed on us. Here's a nugget. ***A product without a label is dangerous to society.*** In a good way so are you; dangerous because you are not categorized and boxed-in by the expectations of people, but are free to become anything you wish to be.

Becoming label-free is vital to working your words and finding your path to personal success. You have to remove the labels of negativity, failure and underachievement that society has placed on you. This is an urgent mental surgery that you must undergo, today! This surgery is critical to your livelihood, your success, and destiny.

FREEDOM TO BE ...

I remember giving a motivational talk to a group of my "inner-city" students in North East Florida, just weeks leading up to their state final exam. Most of them were labeled as failures and a menace to the school environment. Some of who were not expected to do well on the test either.

As I began my talk, I looked around the auditorium at the faces of these young people and my heart became heavy. I could see the hurt, despair and hopelessness placed upon them by societal labeling. I mustered up a few words of encouragement to help them change their thinking. At first, I asked them if they wished to become label-free and they all said, YES! Then I asked them to raise their hands if they believed they could become label-free and hands went up everywhere.

It was from this talk that I coined the phrase *"I am free to be what I want to be...you ain't got no labels on me."* We chanted that phrase vigorously several times over. I then raised my hand to calm them down and get their attention. After they sat down I asked them to close their eyes and think about every hurtful label that was ever placed upon them, voluntarily or not, and together we will remove them on a count of three. The room suddenly seemed charged with emotional baggage. Next, I instructed them to reach across their chests to their outer arm (as if attempting to give themselves a one-handed bear hug) and repeat after me: *"Today I am now label-free; I will open my eyes and rip these labels of burden off of me...*" I stood there in amazement as they ripped those invisible labels of bondage off and set themselves free! I will forever cherish that moment. The students went on to take their tests and a few months ago I received messages that some of those students had scored at the highest levels on the science portion of their state exam. They were now free to be more than labels said they could.

ROOTS AT WORK

One of the greatest structures on earth is the root of a tree. Roots are usually underground and go unnoticed but they are at the top of my list when it comes to function. A root is one of the most determined living structures known to mankind. It exemplifies all the elements of resiliency, adaptability and sheer strength. The roots of a tree are responsible for keeping it standing still, and provide adequate nourishment and water despite the weather. Roots are flexible and persistent enough to travel across the most unlikely places in order to find water to preserve the life of the tree.

At times, you may see cracks in the road which cannot be attributed to climatic conditions affecting the asphalt. It is usually roots that are responsible for redesigning our roadways and transforming the earth's surface. They also maintain landforms and prevent land erosion and soil runoff. ***Roots are tenacious by nature, dependent by function and unique by design. And so are you.*** Is there something in your life that you dream of doing one day? Like roots you must be persistent, determined, and possess the will power to travel to uncharted grounds in order to find the water and bring it back to the trunk of your dreams to make it a reality.

A root never gives up and neither should you. Remember, winners never quit, and quitters never win, but quitters also never discover anything new. Newness is a healthy sign of growth and personal development. Without this many people remain stagnant and unproductive and depreciate over time. Don't let this be your plight.

FUEL FOR YOUR JOURNEY

To work your words you must become internally motivated. Having the right motivation is essential to maintaining your course on the success highway. Your thinking should now be at a higher level as you develop and grow. Keep in mind there may be some rough starts but things will smooth out as you begin to gain some momentum. You are now in the driver's seat and you must be alert. Adjust your speed and remain focused. ***Buckle up with the spirit of perseverance, look forward with determination and make right judgments as you adjust your course with a heart of discernment.*** Do not allow anyone to push your pedal, pump it yourself. Be internally motivated instead of doing things just for external accolades and the eye-pleasing crowd. These are temporary and do fade over time. But if you are internally motivated you will increase your ability to weather the temporary storms of living.

Remember you are branded for personal success first before public approval. You are a gift to the world and your product is how well you use your gift (you, the brand) to influence lives and change the world around you. Be on the alert. As your dream gets closer to materializing, the naysayers will come out of the wood-works to sabotage you. Their only intentions are to kill the dream before it comes to fruition. In the bible story of Jesus' birth, Herod the king was not interested in worshiping the new born king. He wanted to destroy him. In the same manner, your dreams are like a king that will one day save the world, but there are others who will do anything to prevent this from happening even though the very thing they seek to destroy could one day save their lives.

Here's something to help you on your journey. Naysayers are good to have around; you just have to know how to use them to your advantage. They are fuel for your journey to help push and motivate you to achieve.

THE OVEN EXPERIENCE

For many of us, even in our glory-days and climatic achievements, we still have not fully experienced the greatness of our potential. We are like an unbaked cake; not yet finished, but still in the oven waiting for all our ingredients to merge together to produce an amazing taste. And with time, pressure and heat, we will emerge as a delicious cake, ready to be served to the world. Remember, you have everything you need to be great. You and I were made that way, "fearfully and wonderfully created," by the creator.

Mind you, no one likes the oven; it's clustered, hot, uncomfortable, and at times dark and lonely. Like many great men and women in history, you will have to go solo sometimes to see your dreams come true. But rest assured that the one who created you, placed everything inside of you to succeed. However, ***there is a reason for every bruise you endure and a bigger purpose for things you overcome.***

During your trials, like the cake in the oven, it may seem like you are the only one having it hard or feeling the harsh heat. Endure it anyway... Many times others are experiencing something much harder than you. So instead of complaining, always remember that those who feel it know it, and they live to tell the stories too.

When you have been tried, tested and proven true (the process of living) like the well-finished cake, oven-crisp, yet moist (humble) at its center and tasty with every bite; so will the right opportunities meet your preparedness after you have endured the conventionally tormenting heat of the oven (your trials), for a season.

Upon exiting the oven you will develop characteristics that you never had before. For example, you will be a little crispy on the outside; this represents your strength and toughness; the moistened center signifies your temperament to deal with people and the challenges that life may bring; the sweet taste is your reward for being dedicated and faithful to your journey. Never give up!

PACE YOURSELF...ENDURE THE HEAT

One thing is for sure, you cannot rush the process of greatness. Like honey in a bottle, it may take some time to reach the opening but you will get there if you faint not. Your oven experience was meant to bake you into the person you are to become, a product of greatness! Not mediocre, but solid; not watered-down, but highly concentrated and resilient! Not here today, gone tomorrow, but with substance and longevity. Of course, it should be rewarding and not in vain. Remember life is not a race, but there are people who live life as if it is one. Some will quickly utter, "This is my life, and I am in total control. I must do so and so by this time; I must accomplish all my goals (married, kids, job, house, and all that glitters) by a certain age. I can't wait; my biological clock is ticking, I must get there now."

Sounds familiar? Truth is, some may achieve all the above, and even more, but at what price? As the saying goes, "not all that glitters is gold." Not all successes are worth chasing. Some are simply "gold-plated" and without substance. You may look at those shallow people and others like them and say to yourself, "Wow, they are definitely living the life I wish I had!" Or at the very least, you wish you could come close to it.

You may even go as far as to say, "They have everything I wish I had! Gosh! When will my turn come?" Or, "I don't feel like I have done anything worthwhile with my life. I am just a big-flop!"

Remember the universe was created by words, and if you speak negative words, you will have what you say. So speak what you want to happen, not the opposite. Create your world with the right words and find your pathway to success. Be like the roots. Be encouraged! Never give up! Remember quitters never win and winners never quit, but even more, quitters never discover anything new.

Those negative thoughts are only distractions. You are branded for success and the world will see your product and how well you use your gift to change your world. Just keep your focus, and keep reminding yourself that this too will pass, and that you were made for such a time as this.

Never mind the pushers and shovers; pacing yourself is the best thing you can do. Consider this, an over-heated oven will always burn whatever it holds, but one that is regulated with the right temperature might take a while to bake but it always produces a desirable product. A life with anxiety leads to unnecessary disappointments and pain, while patience, timing and dedication produce fruitfulness and success beyond measure.

THE ATTITUDE OF STICK-TO-WITH-IT-NESS

You are called to be strong, no matter the season or weather. So, be open to life (the gift) and to circumstances (the process), for in them lies hope and the building of sheer strength. Never give up; you are closer than you think!

As you begin to transform your mind to thinking bigger, I encourage you to have "***stick-to-with-it-ness***," never quit. Life is simple; it's a blessed gift, but the process of living is your greatest challenge. As I write these words into your hearts, minds and destiny, I am reminded of a life-changing story told by Napoleon Hill, from his book, *Think and Grow Rich*. In it, he spoke of R.U. Darby and his near fortune that became his misfortune.

In summary, Mr. Darby invested a large sum of money after discovering a shining ore in one of the richest mines in Colorado. After drilling desperately without any reward or sign of more shiny ore he called it quits. He packed up his machinery and sold it. Shortly thereafter, the person who bought his equipment got some expert help and used the same machine to find gold just three feet away from where Mr. Darby gave up! Isn't it ironic that the biggest discovery was made in the same location, with same machinery, but with a different attitude? It took persistence. Darby quit just three feet away from striking it rich during the gold-rush era.

Before you quit, think again; what could you be missing that may only be three feet away from your big toe. You may take a break to regroup, but never quit. Use your unsuccessful attempts as lessons-learned to make your future attempts successful. According to Hill, Mr. Darby did just that. He went on to become one of the greatest salesperson of all times. Every day, and every hour, is an opportunity for you to learn. Unlike many of us, Mr. Darby used his unsuccessful attempts and lessons-learned to make him more "stickable" and "unquitable" in his future endeavors.

There is no growth or improvement in the absent of challenges and failed attempts. Challenges make you strong, and avoiding them is like a rehab patient who desires wellness but refuses to do his therapeutic exercises. It makes no sense. Do not give up when things seem too difficult. In the words of Robert H. Schuller, *"Tough times never last but tough people do"*. In the end, quitting will leave you with untapped, undiscovered, and unused potential. Dare to dream and WORK to make it a reality.

POINTS TO PONDER

You are free to become what you want to be...when you become label-free. Remove your labels of oppression and start a new transition as you work your words and create your path to personal success. Never live in regret. Do not look back at your life as a waste. You look back only to measure your progress and how far you've come. And if you have come this far, then you should know by now that you have everything inside of you to be ALL that you were created to be. Indeed, you and I were created to be people of excellence; nothing less. Therefore, if you settle for less you would've short-changed yourself and accepted the crumbs which fell to the ground instead of feasting at the table of life.

CHAPTER SEVEN

PEOPLE WHO FOUND THEIR PATHWAYS: Supplementary tips for Teachers & Educators

"We never stop living until quitting becomes a way of life."
~Andrew E. Guy

NOTES

PEOPLE WHO FOUND THEIR PATHWAYS:
Supplementary tips for Teachers & Educators

Microsoft chairperson and CEO, Bill Gates along with Apple's founder, Steve Jobs are both examples of men who left the "out-there" to pursue something bigger, and more lasting that would change the way the world views success. Both Microsoft and Apple are among some of the most powerful trend-setting tech companies today. And all because of leaders who refused to be counted among the world's way of dreaming; they worked their words to make the "in-there" success became a personal reality for everyone who's ever used a computer.

What about you? When will you start thinking outside of this "boxed-in" mind-set, and begin a new journey on the pathway that leads to real tangible, freedom-living success? By the way, the "boxed-in" mindset cripples, stifles, and robs you of any possibility of personal success and victorious living. Get out of the box. Jump if you have to. Do it now. Today is your day. Embrace the challenges and begin today.

There are countless examples of extraordinary success pioneers to help motivate you along your path as you work your words to discover personal success.

Remember Benjamin Carson, the so-called 'dumbest boy' in his entire middle school; who, under the guidance of his resilient mother, traded in his television watching for a pair of bi-focal glasses, some well-deserved library time, some high-class spelling skills, and some obsidian rocks, to become Dr. Ben Carson, MD., the first black pediatric neurosurgeon ever to separate conjoined twins? He jumped out of his box; in fact, his mother pushed him and his brother out of the box, burned it and buried the ashes forever. It's your turn now...

This section would not be complete if I did not mention Michael Jordan, the "Air Up There." Most knew him as his "Airness." Here is a young black man who did not make his high school basketball team. Yet he persevered to become one of the world's greatest athletes in the game of basketball.

His freedom of success did not come the world's way; neither did he look "out-there" for it; he simply, looked "in-there," inside himself and then gave us a glimpse of what he saw—The "Air Up There."

You are now without excuse... Go! Do it over. Your dreams are not BIG ENOUGH, nor did you aim HIGH ENOUGH, looked LONG and FAR ENOUGH, nor have you thought DEEP ENOUGH... Go! Do it over...and then go get 'em!

Remember, your success is first personal before it becomes public. When you become great at what you do, when you do what you do, like no one else can do, when you do it one hundred percent wholeheartedly, your personal success becomes publicly known and you are remembered for what you do, as you did what you said, when you worked your words.

Now your pathway to success must become a trailblazing light in a dark world. Your success is not just necessary in the grand scheme of things, it is vital. What would the world be if those before us abandoned their success like an unwanted fetus? And what would the world of computers be without the likes of Bill Gates and Steve Jobs? Just imagine!

So what about you? What are you looking at? Are you measuring your self-worth by the world's system? And, are you seeing what you're supposed to see? Do you see yourself as a success? If not, you are looking in the wrong direction and working the wrong plan for your life.

AN EDUCATOR'S PATH TO SUCCESS

> *"It is not your lesson plan or instructions
> that matters most, but your intentions…"*
> ~Andrew E. Guy

As a science teacher in North Florida, USA, I often read to my students every afternoon, especially to the teenage boys who were troublesome. I recall, quite vividly, after reading the "Gifted Hands" by Dr. Ben Carson, that most of the students sitting in the back of the classroom had tears in their eyes. Especially after reading the part when little Bennie had to deal with the fact that his daddy was never coming back anymore to live with them.

Not only did I read to them, I was one of those "cool-science-teachers" (CST) who did everything to make the lesson interesting enough for even the most challenging students to become engaged and want to listen. As a matter of fact, I did above and beyond what a really "cool-science-teachers" (CST) should do. Plus, I have come to learn that it does not matter if you have the best lesson plan or deliver the greatest lesson in your classroom; effective student engagement and meaningful instructions matters most when you have the right intentions. Sometimes I can be firm with my students and they would say, "Mr. Guy, you're MEAN...!" No; not mean, but WELL...I MEAN YOU WELL!

I set my standards and expectations very high; that way it would take the class all semester to reach it. I figured by doing it this way there would always be something for the students to shoot for other than just a basketball hoop-dream.

Next, I would do everything to try and create a positive environment for students to feel empowered enough to open up and discuss their issues. And believe me there were many of those. I even started an activity called *"Get It Out...Real Talk."* This was a live discussion that allowed students to vent, question, break, and mend relationships with their classmates. Sometimes it got a little chaotic and I was left to play the part of judge and jury, but we always managed to end on a positive note.

To promote productivity and personal growth in my class, I gave every student a responsibility. Our approach was similar to a corporation. Each period had specific duties to accomplish every class. Some of their responsibilities included:

secretary, lab coordinator, materials personnel, clean-up crew, data collections, small group leaders, study-buddies, homework collectors, test graders, dress code advisors, one for boys and one for girls; we also had student peer-counselors, these would serve as stress relief aid when another student was having personal difficulties that she may not wish to discuss with me. It was our little business and we took it seriously every day.

To address the absentee issues, I came up with this idea of a virtual classroom call *NEVER MISS A DAY IN MR. GUY'S CLASS*. After each class I would create video summary lessons of all the content we discussed that day, edit and post it on my teacher's website, and then use them as homework or extra credit points. For those students who missed a day, I allowed them time after they finished the day's work to sit in the back of the class at a computer with earphones and take notes. It worked wonders, and made teaching much easier for me. Most of the students thought I was some kind of superstar on television because they watched me on the computer.

As I began to *WORK MY WORDS* to create my success I realized that I had to do things differently, and as naturally as I saw fit. So in addition to creating crazy voices while reading Dr. Carson's books to my students, I would also challenge them to do well on my tests and if they did, the highest scores above eighty-five percent (85%) would play Mr. Guy (me) in a one-on-one basketball game. They took me up on that challenge, and this became the driving force that assisted me in helping my students overcome tough days and caused them to think outside of the neighborhood walls of their inner city lives.

The games were held mostly on Fridays after school. There would be over a dozen young men waiting to play basketball in the gymnasium. We played for hours, and they behaved well too because they knew my standards were high, I took no nonsense, and I genuinely cared for them. I developed a great rapport with my students. Whenever I would pass them in the hallways or in the cafeteria at lunchtimes, I gave the girls hi-fives and fist-pounds or daps to the boys.

I took a keen interest in their personal lives and sought ways to help motivate them in and outside of the classroom. Frankly, it didn't matter whose class they were in. I would make it my duty to speak with the students, or that teacher, especially if they were in my class. Most times they never had to worry if they did not have a pencil or sheet of paper to write on. I would always remind them before they enter that, to be successful you must have the tools of success. I would then say to each of them, like a broken record that spins on its axis every day, *"You must have something to write with and something to write on."* I had much buy-ins and some slow starters but we made it work.

Other times I would observe when my students were having difficulties outside of the classroom, and I would set aside some time to chat with them. This was important to me because I have learned that **classroom management has little to do with the internal operations of a classroom, but more or less, the sequence of events that goes on outside the four walls.** If you can manage the external forces the internal behaviors would diminish significantly. Great teachers become evident when they care more about the lives they touch than the subject matter they teach.

I would seek out ways to encourage and empower my students. I would impress upon them the importance of using proper vernacular and the power of using words correctly. Hence the title of this book: WORK YOUR WORDS. The evidence of your reward will be based on the words you speak. Work the right ones and lives will change, but speak the wrong ones and dreams will die. The youth of today are the future of tomorrow, and if we neglect to see that now, then our visions of sustaining life on earth is dark and dismal.

As part of my quest to improve their vocabulary, I came up with this concept call "W.O.T.S." also known as "Words On The Street." The overall purpose of this was to influence their street vernacular by incorporating science vocabulary terms from our lesson that they should use outside of my class. The students would then earn points if they could use the terms in a complete sentence outside of the classroom. We also used "W.O.T.S." to prepare for quizzes, tests, and end of term exams, and guess what? It worked.

Additionally, I would create videos of their presentations and then have them watch it and analyze it for improvement. You knew you were in Mr. Guy's Science class when you entered because there would be posters and an array of students' work decorating the classroom walls. I would make posters of important vocabulary, equations, and key science terms along with mnemonic devices to aid their memory. This was a "B.I.G." help to them. It improved their learning and retention tremendously.

Above and beyond that, I would ask permission from the principal to do motivational speeches and workshops to help my students. I showed up at their athletics and band practices, and performed the opening skit for their championship drum-off for BILL COSBY at the Florida Times Union Theater. I also provided physical activities to help them perform better at their chosen sport, lead study halls to improve their grades, and even helped tie a few neckties on special occasions. They would say, "Mr. Guy, can you hook me up?" That means, can you help me tie my tie, sir? I would stop whatever I was doing to assist. I took much pride in doing this since I too, had two young boys less than six years and I could see myself teaching them how to tie their first neckties. This was practice for me and I cherished it.

Other times they would say, "Mr. Guy, I really like that tie you got on. Can I have it?" I wasted no time; off it went and on their necks. Some wore it for the rest of the entire day. This tradition went on for quite some time until I started buying ties to give away to my students. I really wanted them to see that all things are possible, and I was willing to do my part and lead by example. I held nothing back. I gave it everything I had, including a dollar or two, if the need was genuine. I would reward them by buying pizzas, chicken wings and drinks. A portion of my paycheck was dedicated to feeding my students. And they enjoyed every moment of it.

One of my class mottos was, "You are never done until you've helped someone." This was my way of teaching them the principles of effective teamwork and how to build stronger communities. As a result, many of my students began studying more and helping each other with science equations, vocabulary and reading strategies. And even though some teachers regard their paychecks as their primary sign of success, I disagree; to me this was success. It was personal success because I gave it everything to create a mindset and a pathway for my students to follow. After leaving the profession, I received messages from parents, teachers and those students telling me how well they did on the State exam. And yes, some successes can get you choked up, just a little bit...

BRING THE POWER OF SUCCESS PATHWAYS
TO YOUR ORGANIZATION:

WORK YOUR WORDS

WORKSHOP

Empowerment, Energy, and an Entrepreneurial spirit are just some of the possibilities when youth, employees and organizations experience the *WORK YOUR WORDS©* onsite workshop. Your team will be inspired to develop individual success pathways that will transform every aspect of their lives.

WORK YOUR WORDS to become more conscious of the words they speak, improve communication and build stronger relationships to optimal teamwork.

WORK YOUR WORDS to build self-confidence, improve self-esteem, improve wellness initiatives and become more productive in everyday living.

WORK YOUR WORDS WORKSHOP is customized to suit the needs of your organization.

This workshop is fun, interactive and provides hands-on demos to propel your group to success.

WORK YOUR WORDS **Workshop** is ideal for the following:

- Corporate workshops and new hires
- Youth conferences and seminars
- Onsite employee training
- Students and educators
- Student athletes
- Teacher training and Professional Development
- Government employees
- Public works department and Police
- Military and civilian personnel
- Small businesses and Entrepreneurs

ABOUT THE AUTHOR

Andrew Guy is a multi-gifted individual who empowers people to improve character, dream big, build meaningful relationships, and discover their unique gifts provided to better themselves and others. Andrew is a certified 2nd DAN Black Belt Martial Arts Instructor, Certified Science Educator, Preventive Health & Wellness Specialist, speaker, trainer, a father and husband. He attended Southern Arkansas University (SAU) where he obtained his Masters of Science degree.

Andrew served as president of the International Students Association (ISA) where he implemented programs and activities that earned him a student leadership merit award from the University's President, Dr. David Rankin.

He has participated in regular television and radio programs, facilitated teacher development sessions on classroom technology and effective student engagement and has also served as a

Presenter at the **Magnet Schools of America in Tulsa, Oklahoma**, a National Conference for Educators, and campus leaders.

Today, Andrew is an author, speaker, and a wellness consultant. As an international empowerment speaker, Andrew provides a high-energy interactive experience that is tailor-made to fit your program needs. It is time well spent and filled with laughter, motivation and on-time inspiration to empower his audience. Andrew's approach to empowering people makes him unique. He's a blend of humor, inspiration and advise with easy to understand nuggets that you can apply to your life. You can be confident when booking Andrew for your next event that both you and your audience will be glad he was there. For more information visit www.AndrewGuySpeaks.com

www.ingramcontent.com/pod-product-compliance
Lightning Source LLC
Chambersburg PA
CBHW060205100426
42744CB00007B/1179